Original title:
Gravity's Punchline

Copyright © 2025 Creative Arts Management OÜ
All rights reserved.

Author: Gabriel Kingsley
ISBN HARDBACK: 978-1-80567-866-3
ISBN PAPERBACK: 978-1-80567-987-5

Exhale into the Abyss

In the depths of a dizzy sky,
I waved my feet goodbye.
The ground took one sly glance,
And I began my bouncy dance.

A bird laughed at my plight,
As I soared in pure delight.
Falling soft like a feather,
The clouds and I shared a tether.

The Leap of Levity

I took a leap with great cheer,
Imagining I'd veer.
With each upward glance,
I found my pants in a trance.

The stars clapped, oh so bright,
As I stumbled mid-flight.
The universe spun in glee,
While I considered my next spree.

The Gentle Tumble

Down I fell with a chuckle,
An accidental shuffle.
The ground met my behind,
Wrote laughter in my mind.

Roses below shared a grin,
As I landed with a spin.
Nature giggled in the breeze,
While I begged, "Oh, not the knees!"

Celestial Laugh Tracks

Stars twinkled with mischievous grins,
As the cosmos played violin spins.
With a flip and a twist,
I joined their cosmic list.

Planets chuckled in their round,
As I floated off the ground.
In this dance of silly fate,
I found joy in my lightweight state.

Laughing Through the Abyss

Falling up instead of down,
Jokes collide in a wide frown.
The ground laughs as I float by,
In the void, it's hard to cry.

Witty puns defy all sense,
In the air, there's no pretense.
I trip on dreams, they make me grin,
Even when I know I'll spin.

A Weighty Reprieve

Heavy hearts, they try to soar,
Slipping past the open door.
With every leap, a comic fall,
Laughter echoes, bouncing ball.

Floating on a giggling puff,
Life's a jest, and that's enough.
The punchline lands, a gentle thud,
Tickling toes in a moonlit flood.

The Velocity of Joy

Speeding through this fickle air,
Joy spins around without a care.
With every twist, a silly slip,
Life's a ride, don't lose your grip.

Up and down, we sway and sway,
Joking 'bout the fall away.
Descent's a dance, a merry spree,
Joy whirls all around, so free.

Gravity's Hidden Chuckle

In the depths where shadows play,
A silent joke makes darkness sway.
When I stumble, it's no waste,
The ground grins, it's all in haste.

Bouncing high like a rubber ball,
Life's got puns that enthrall.
With every plummet, I just laugh,
It's the universe's playful math.

The Subtle Weight of Joy

In the dance of a balloon,
One twist sends it aloft.
Why does it drift like a loon,
Escaping with all of its soft?

A feather floats by with sass,
Defying all sense of bound.
We watch as it swirls and it clasps,
Then lands gently onto the ground.

A cat leaps for the sky,
With grace that makes all hearts race.
But fails to catch all that high,
And lands in a comical place.

Joy doesn't fumble or fall,
It bounces on laughter's wing.
Just like a kid with a ball,
It's all giggles, no serious thing.

Laughter's Landing

When the world spins in jest,
Frogs wear ties on a lane.
They croak as if they're the best,
Their elegance is insane.

A dog with a stick in his mouth,
Charges forth like a knight.
But trips on his tail, oh, south!
He rolls in a whirl of delight.

The sun shines with a wink,
As clouds puff up in a cheer.
They sprout laughter before we think,
Dropping joy, not a tear.

Each step leads to a giggle,
Life's quirks take center stage.
In moments where we wiggle,
We find laughter's sweet gauge.

Aerial Antics

A squirrel on a branch so wide,
Waves to a bird on the fly.
Then jumps for a ride, pure pride,
And tumbles with a surprise.

Kites soar high with bright tails,
Chasing dreams in the breeze.
But one takes flight without fails,
Fighting knots with such ease.

When kids run, arms open wide,
They spin like crazy tops.
Unplanned tumbles, pure joy inside,
As laughter continuously pops.

A butterfly takes a chance,
Dancing on a breeze with flair.
But mid-flight, it sings a prance,
And lands where nobody's aware.

The Pull of the Silly

Two socks dare to tango,
Waltzing without a care.
One slips on a jangle,
While others simply stare.

An old clown trips in style,
His shoes honking with glee.
The crowd bursts into a smile,
As he bows with a flair for free.

A fish on a skateboard rolls,
Seeking waves in the street.
He flips and swirls, all the goals,
And then lands on his tail, oh sweet!

Life's quirks are a twisty ride,
Where the greatest humor plays.
In each stumble and glide,
Lies a laugh that forever stays.

Whispers from the Edge

A bird took a dive, what a sight,
It landed on a branch, felt just right.
Then slipped on some leaves, oh what a mess,
It twirled in the air, with a clumsy finesse.

A squirrel ran to catch, what a brave face,
Tripped on a twig, then fell from grace.
With a flip and a flop, that little guy flew,
Landed on a road, declared it a zoo!

A dog jumped to fetch, oh what a chase,
But slipped on his shadow, lost all his pace.
He rolled and he tumbled, a sight to behold,
The laughter erupted, pure joy uncontrolled.

A cat on a fence, so proud and so sly,
Spotted a butterfly, said, "I can fly!"
It leapt for the catch, but found only air,
Flopped on the grass, got tangled in flair.

Colliding Worlds of Humor

An ant on a hill thought he could soar,
A leaf on the breeze, his trusty galore.
He climbed to the top, took a leap with a grin,
And fell with a plop, what a world he was in!

A kitten so brave, with dreams of the skies,
Chased after a moth, oh what a surprise.
It leapt for the catch, but missed by a mile,
Tumbled head over heels, yet smiled all the while.

A frog on a log, croaked loud, took a chance,
Hopped into space, started a dance.
But the gravity giggles pulled him right back,
He landed back down, on the soft grassy pack.

A cow in the field had a fanciful thought,
"Why not join the birds?" she happily sought.
She leapt from the ground, with a moo-ving embrace,
But flopped on her side, rolled with the grace.

Bouncing on Serendipity

In the park, a duck takes flight,
Chasing crumbs, oh what a sight!
The baker's hat, it soars so high,
Butterflies giggle, oh my, oh my!

While on swings, we twist and spin,
Who knew laughter could be such a win?
A leap of faith in the funniest way,
We float like clouds, brightening the day!

The Interstellar Giggle

A rocket made of yesterday's cheese,
Explores the cosmos with utmost ease.
Stars wink back, and planets tease,
What a ride, oh sweet galactic breeze!

Floating past Mars, an alien sings,
With every laugh, a whole universe swings.
Jokes echo down the Milky Way tight,
Where even comets chuckle in flight!

Roots of Wit

In the garden where puns grow tall,
A radish whispered, "I won't fall!"
The carrots chuckled, or so they said,
"We dig deep down, never a dread!"

A joke-telling flower blooms with cheer,
Releasing giggles that all can hear.
Roots entwined, they share and play,
Creating joy in their leafy ballet!

Starlit Echoes of Laughter

Under stars that wink and blink,
We share our thoughts, we laugh, we think.
A comet zooms with a silly grin,
While moonbeams dance, inviting us in.

A barista asteroid brews up a storm,
With spacetime coffee that's out of norm.
Sip and snicker, the sky is alive,
In this cosmic realm, our chuckles thrive!

The Nimbus of Jest

In a cloud of giggles bright,
Up high where laughs take flight,
Raindrops turn to comedy,
As puddles hold a symphony.

Each tumble from the sky,
A joke just passing by,
With every splash and cheer,
Life's quirks draw us near.

So ride on fluffy dreams,
Where silliness redeems,
Laughter's weightless grace,
Brings smiles to every face.

Amid the jests we spin,
Let's embrace the whim within,
For every fall we take,
Is just a chance to wake!

Silly in the Slipstream

A comet's tail, so bright and bold,
Zips by with giggles untold,
In the slipstream of delight,
Every wink's a sparkling light.

Bananas float in neon air,
While flying pies declare,
That laughter's faster still,
In a world that's high on thrill.

Wobble and mingle, twist and shout,
As jokes fly like a friendly bout,
With every swoop and dive,
The silly keeps us alive.

Through the cosmic dance we glide,
With chuckles as our guide,
In a universe of fun,
An endless race that's just begun!

The Teeter of Timelessness

On a seesaw of delight,
We bounce through day and night,
With time stretched like a rubber band,
Where funny quirks simply stand.

Each tick and tock's a jester's call,
As moments rise and fall,
Like rubber chickens in a race,
They land with a comical grace.

In the wobbly dance we sway,
With every laugh we play,
Defying what we know,
In a farcical flow.

So gather 'round with glee to see,
The joy of jesting, wild and free,
For in this timeless tease,
We giggle with such ease!

Witty Wonders in Freefall

With a leap into the air,
We float without a care,
Finding wit in every twist,
Where gravity's a playful mist.

Jokes hover like balloons,
Chatters dance 'neath silver moons,
As we tumble without fear,
Each chuckle pulls us near.

Hearts race in the comic spree,
As laughter sets us free,
Every flutter brings a grin,
In the joy where we begin.

So drop into the fun we make,
Let every giggle shake,
In freefall, light and bold,
Our stories dare to unfold!

The Arch of Delight

In a world where apples fall,
And heads turn when they call.
The moon winks at sneaky stars,
While planets giggle from afar.

Jupiter spins in oversized shoes,
While Saturn plays its ringed blues.
A tickle behind each cosmic play,
With laughter echoing through the fray.

Comets zoom in carefree flights,
As asteroids join in silly fights.
The sun beams with a golden grin,
While space dances, let the fun begin!

With humor woven through the skies,
The universe wears its jokester guise.
As Mrs. Earth tries to hold her drink,
She stumbles, and all the neighbors wink.

The Chorus of the Cosmos

Stars compose a merry tune,
Singing loud beneath the moon.
The planets join in happy throng,
Each one clapping to the song.

Shooting stars take gallant bows,
While black holes chuckle, 'What? Our vows?'
The Milky Way sways side to side,
With cosmic comedies as its guide.

Quasars flicker with bright delight,
As cosmic rays bring laughter's light.
Comets racing through the scene,
Spreading giggles, bright and keen.

In every corner of the vast sky,
Laughter dances, lifting high.
For in this cosmic, funny play,
Who knew stardust could make your day?

Gravity's Delightful Secrets

In the realm of up and down,
Balloons escape with a frown.
While socks vanish, with a wink,
They float away, and we just think!

Belly laughs from the ground below,
As boulders roll and flowers grow.
Each tumble, a giggle, a bouncy cheer,
What funny tricks, from here to near!

Lunar leaps and Martian hops,
In a dance where nobody stops.
The gravity of humor keeps us light,
Turning frowns to smiles so bright.

With each fall, a chuckle traced,
In the merry mix of space embraced.
Here's to the humor without a plan,
As the universe plays its trickster hand!

Dancing with the Comet

Come join the comet on its flight,
With trails of laughter, pure delight.
It zips and zooms through dusk and dawn,
Leaving giggles that linger on.

In the galaxy's vibrant ball,
Where wobbling worlds can hardly stand tall.
They sway with joy and spin with glee,
The cosmos humming a quirky decree.

Nebulas twist in playful cheer,
While suns wink through every sphere.
The asteroid band starts to play,
As stars dance in a wild ballet.

So grab a partner, take the chance,
Join the stars in a cosmic dance.
For in this space of fun and jest,
Life's little punchlines are truly the best!

Floating on Sarcasm

In a world where puns take flight,
I trip on thoughts that seem so light.
Bouncing quips like rubber balls,
   I laugh as logic takes a fall.

Every step, a comic grace,
As wit and wisdom interlace.
I juggle lines with careless zest,
   In this circus, I'm the jest.

The higher I get, the funnier it seems,
Each smile erupts from tired dreams.
With air beneath my carefree feet,
   I dance and jest, life is a treat.

In this paradox where truths collide,
I float on sarcasm, full of pride.
With every slip, a chance to play,
   I laugh at life, come what may.

Hilarity in the Echo

Whispers bounce like rubber ducks,
Filling spaces with silly clucks.
An echo laughs in mimicry,
As I join in the reverie.

Chasing shadows, we collide,
With punchlines that we can't abide.
The walls are laughing, can't you hear?
While echoes dress in comic cheer.

In this chamber of sound and jest,
Each chuckle's a contest, who's the best?
Raindrops giggle, the pavement sighs,
As laughter dances through the skies.

Every sound is a playful tease,
Unraveling woes with effortless ease.
In this hall of echoes and mirth,
I find the joy that springs from earth.

The Stillness of a Jest

In quiet moments, humor hides,
Like a snail in a shell that glides.
Stillness holds a punchline tight,
Waiting to burst with pure delight.

Serious faces have no clue,
That laughter's just a breath or two.
I catch the smiles that wander near,
In the silence, jokes appear.

A pause before the giggles soar,
An unexpected laugh at the door.
As I stand still with a tethered grin,
The jest reveals the joy within.

So here I'll wait in still repose,
For the tickle that erupts and grows.
In the calm, the fun has space,
To stretch and leap, in comical grace.

Celestial Guffaws

Stars wink down with playful glare,
As comets zoom with flair to spare.
The universe conspires to jest,
With every twinkle, life's a fest.

Planets dance in cosmic mirth,
Spinning tales of joy and worth.
Nebulas burst in colors bright,
As galaxies giggle through the night.

In the expanse, where laughter's free,
Gravity's not invited, you see.
With every orbit, worlds collide,
A symphony of fun worldwide.

So let us laugh beneath the sky,
With cosmic punchlines soaring high.
For in this vast and lively spree,
The stars and I, in sync, agree.

The Attraction of Absurdity

In a world where apples fall,
Bananas giggle, having a ball.
Cows on trampolines, leap so spry,
While frogs wear hats, oh my oh my!

Squirrels debate in the trees up high,
Who can juggle acorns and sky?
The dance of the odd, it's quite a sight,
As fish on bicycles take flight!

With every twirl and silly laugh,
They plot their next comedic gaffe.
Laughter floats on bubbles of cheer,
In this wacky realm, no fear is near!

So let's embrace the glorious jest,
In the circus of quirks, we're truly blessed.
For in this dance of the odd and funny,
Life's but a joke, and joy is our honey!

Laughter's Tug of War

Two giggling giants pull on a rope,
While clouds wear frowns, unable to cope.
Tickles abound in the gentle breeze,
As turtles try running with utmost ease.

The sun grins wide, its rays a tease,
Flicking shadows that wiggle with ease.
A race with the wind, a chase for delight,
As balloons drift past, oh what a sight!

With each hearty chuckle, the world spins round,
The joy of the jest in every sound.
Jellybeans in pockets, candy in the air,
In this tug of joy, we share and we stare.

So let's play and jest, with laughter we'll soar,
For humor's the thread that binds us for sure.
In this playful game where nothing's a bore,
We'll giggle and wiggle, and always want more!

When the Universe Smiles

Stars twinkle with mischief in the night,
While comets play tag, a dazzling flight.
Planets wear hats that are silly and bright,
And moons share jokes with a wink of delight.

A galaxy spins in a dance of glee,
While black holes joke, "Come play with me!"
The cosmos chuckles, expands with grace,
As meteors race in a comical chase.

With each little laugh, the stardust sways,
Creating bright trails in whimsical ways.
The universe hums a joyous tune,
Where laughter blooms like flowers in June.

So let's join this cosmic, joyous scheme,
For laughter's the thread that connects every dream.
In a galaxy filled with humor and light,
We'll dance through the stars, shimmering bright!

The Antics of Ascendancy

Up the hill, the ants parade,
With tiny trumpets, they serenade.
Wobbling upward with all their might,
As grasshoppers join in, what a sight!

A curious cloud drips sprinkles of fun,
While pigeons compete in a race to the sun.
Little mice squabble over who can glide,
On paper airplanes that float and ride.

The breeze shares secrets that tickle the nose,
As blossoms burst forth, in chaotic pose.
A jest from the wind sends squirrels in a spin,
Launching acorns, let the prank wars begin!

In this place where laughter reigns supreme,
Life's but a jest, a whimsical dream.
So grab a friend, let the antics unfold,
In this merry world, let's be bold!

The Balance of Wit

In a world where laughs collide,
And the laws of jest abide,
The punchlines soar and slide,
Bouncing off with mirthful pride.

Like acrobats in midair,
They tumble without a care,
Tickling truth with every glare,
In this balance, we all share.

Slips and trips bring grins anew,
A pratfall now seems overdue,
We laugh until our faces blue,
Life's a circus, join the queue.

So gather round for comic plays,
As laughter lights our silly ways,
With every twist that humor sways,
We'll dance beneath absurd displays.

Comedic Collisions

Two clowns on a busy street,
Each trip they make's a funny feat,
With flying pies, they can't be beat,
Their blunders turn to comic heat.

When jokes collide like crashing cars,
A giggle train that's full of stars,
Their laughter echoes, near and far,
As we watch them slip on candy bars.

In this world of silly sights,
Where pratfalls turn to pure delights,
The joy of humor ignites,
Like fireworks on Christmas nights.

So let's embrace the fumbles bold,
As stories of laughter unfold,
In this game of joy retold,
The fun of life is ours to hold.

Falling Stars and Smiling Hearts

When stars above begin to fall,
They land with laughter, one and all,
With each descent a funny call,
They roll and bounce, oh what a ball!

A space-time giggle, shining bright,
Turns frowns to grins with sheer delight,
With cosmic jokes that take flight,
In this universe, everything's right.

Smiling hearts float in the air,
Like balloons that dance without a care,
In this web of wit so rare,
Humor wraps us in joy's glare.

So catch those stars, don't let them go,
Embrace the laughter, let it flow,
For in this dance of hearts aglow,
We find happiness in the show.

The Pull of Humor

There's a force that makes us laugh,
A cosmic giggle, a silly half,
It tugs and pulls, a joyous path,
In the realm of whimsy, feel the gaffe.

Like a rubber band stretched too far,
The jokes snap back, oh how we spar,
With every pun, we raise the bar,
In this playful universe we are.

As witticisms take their flight,
They swirl and twist in pure delight,
Pulling us close, holding us tight,
In the comedy of day and night.

So give in to that pulling cheer,
Let laughter echo, loud and clear,
In the pull of humor, we find dear,
A world where joy and jest adhere.

Falling into Humor

A jester trips, the crowd's delight,
Banana peel, a classic sight.
He swirls and twirls, a slip so grand,
The whole room laughs, they can't withstand.

With every tumble, laughter bursts,
Like popcorn popping, fun rehearsed.
He somersaults, defying fate,
Who knew that falls could be so great?

A funny face, a bouncing joy,
He winks at fate, a playful ploy.
His pratfalls shine, a comic art,
The punchline wraps around the heart.

The Gravitational Smile

A seeker of joy, he leaps with glee,
But soon finds earth has plans for thee.
He floats on dreams, so light, so spry,
Then down he goes, a comical sigh.

His grin remains, a silly tease,
Catching laughter like a breeze.
Up and down, like a pogo stick,
Life tumbles by, what a fun trick!

Each fall, a giggle, a dance with fate,
As friends all gather to celebrate.
In mops or wipes, they share the cheer,
For every slip, they're always near.

Tension Meets Tickles

A game of balance, a tightrope dare,
One little wobble, and—whoosh!—air.
He teeters, giggles fill the space,
As gravity pulls with a wink on its face.

Finally down in a feathery heap,
He laughs so hard, can't help but weep.
A lesson learned, or maybe not,
That ticklish fall? The best of plot!

With every stumble, joy's the prize,
The frown flips quick to bright surprise.
Life tosses knocks, yet cheer prevails,
In wobbly walks and funny tales.

The Sweetness of the Drop

A child's leap from the backyard swing,
Into soft grass, what joy it brings.
She flutters high, then says, "Oh dear!"
As down she swoops, no hint of fear.

What fun it is to crash and roll,
A happy landing, a freed-up soul.
Laughter echoes through the sunny air,
No time for worries, no need for care.

With ice cream cones, all smiles spread,
Her night of giggles, a dream thread.
A gravity game, so sweet, so fraught,
Laughter springs from the joy she sought.

The Tension of Being

I tried to float, but down I go,
Like a balloon that's lost its glow.
I laughed so hard, I hit the ground,
In every fall, a joy I found.

The tighter I hold, the harder I fall,
It's a comedy that grips us all.
Each stumble feels like life's own play,
In tripping, oh, the fun's on display!

With gravity's pull, we tease the fate,
Like clowns in motion, we can't be late.
Every tumble's a punch of cheer,
In laughter's weight, we persevere.

So dance and roll, let the world see,
The jester's heart, oh so carefree.
We'll take a leap, and then we'll fall,
In life's grand joke, we play it all.

Falls of Euphoria

I leapt into the air with glee,
But gravity said, "Not with me!"
With every bounce, the earth did grin,
My laughter echoed, a joyful din.

Through flips and trips, I sat in bliss,
With every tumble, not a miss.
I danced with air, but down I swept,
In gravity's hug, my heart has leapt.

The world spins round, I spin with it,
As slip-ups make life's comedy hit.
Touched down again, safe and sound,
In this wacky ride, joys abound.

So let's embrace this merry fall,
And find the humor in it all.
There's euphoria in every slip,
In laughter's grip, we freely trip.

Celestial Puns

The stars above are having fun,
As I get pulled by gravity's run.
I twirl and whirl, then trip astray,
A cosmic giggle leads the way.

Planets chuckle, comets cheer,
As I float headfirst without fear.
In every fall, a joke unfolds,
In this vast play, new tales are told.

With every tumble, stars align,
Their laughter echoes, pure divine.
The universe plays a witty game,
In life's grand circus, we're all the same.

So let me soar, then take a dive,
In cosmic jokes, we feel alive.
From the heavens, jokes rain down,
In silly grace, we wear a crown.

The Gravitational Jest

I took a step, then took a dive,
Oh, how it feels to be alive!
My feet went flying, my head did too,
With every fall, the laughter grew.

In every leap, a whimsy awaits,
Like a jester at the door of fate.
I tripped on clouds, I danced with glee,
In each fail, I'm wild and free.

Slipped on a dream, oh what a sight,
My stumbles shine in the pale moonlight.
This jest we share brings souls together,
In laughter's grip, we float forever.

So here's to falls, and here's to fun,
In this grand jest, we're never done.
With every splat, life takes a turn,
In joy's embrace, we always learn.

Fractured Upward

I tripped on air, my feet took flight,
The ceiling's now my newfound height.
My shoes are laughing, they feel so bold,
As I spiral up, with tales retold.

The sun looks down, can't help but grin,
As I somersault, in joyful spin.
A rocket's roar? Just my sneeze's might,
Who knew that skyward was my delight?

I wave to planets, do they see me?
An astronaut's life? Not meant to be.
With every flip, I lose my place,
So back to earth—I start the race.

Finally landing, with a thud and roll,
The right side up, I pay my toll.
Did I just float, or was it a dream?
Up in the clouds, I truly beam.

The Joke in Free Fall

I dropped a pie from high above,
It landed flat, the birds will love!
A pastry splash, a cherry cheer,
Comedic timing, I hold it dear.

A gopher laughs, with crumbs in paw,
"Next time, aim for someone's jaw!"
Gravity pulls, but so does the pie,
In this free fall, no need to fly.

My friend's hat took an unexpected flight,
Spinning through air, quite a sight!
'Catch it!' I yell, but burst into glee,
As it floats away, so wild and free.

Down comes the hat, or should I say feast?
Life's little pranks, its perfect least.
With laughter loud, the sky does call,
In this great fall, we're all in thrall.

The Earth's Subtle Tickle

Stand still, dear friend, and take a glance,
At the ground below, it starts to dance.
A little shiver, a playful tease,
Shaking fingers like a playful breeze.

"Tickle tickle," it whispers near,
As I shuffle about, filled with cheer.
A misstep sends me on a roll,
Tumbling down—what a comic toll!

The daisies giggle, the grass does sway,
As I tripped on my own two feet today.
The ants are cheering, a parade of sorts,
Celebrating falls, like gravity courts.

So leap with joy, don't mind the slide,
For earth's little tickles, we take in stride.
With every tumble, laughter ignites,
As we spin and turn, chased by delights.

Balancing on a Banana Peel

There lay a peel, a bright yellow trap,
I stepped right on it with a little clap.
Was it a dance? Or a clownish act?
In my wild tango, I lost that pact.

Up in the air, what a sight to see!
My pirouette was surely too free.
Spinning and flailing, my feet went high,
A dizzying drop—oh me, oh my!

The world did laugh, it had its fun,
As I grappled with fate, while on the run.
Just like a child, in playful retreat,
I landed softly, with wobbly feet.

All's well that ends, or does it start?
In all of this, I play my part.
So watch your step, take care with zeal,
Or you may find yourself in a squeaky reel.

A Jester's Orbit

In a world where giggles spin,
The jester dances, cheeky grin.
With each stumble, laughter flies,
A spark that tickles, brightens skies.

He juggles hopes, a laugh or two,
Trips on banter, who knew it flew?
Falling fast with jokes in tow,
He lands with joy, steals the show.

Bouncing high on silly schemes,
Reality's laughter, woven dreams.
In this circus, where wit takes flight,
Comedic gravity holds us tight.

So join the spin, take a chance,
In a cartwheel of pure romance.
For every slip, there's mirth to find,
In this rollercoaster of the mind.

The Bottomless Well of Humor

Peering deep in laughter's trench,
Endless echoes, a silly wrench.
Each joke a drop, a splash, a tease,
Filling hearts with giggles, ease.

Down we tumble, no fear at all,
Into the well with a joyful call.
Witty whispers bounce around,
In this cavern, delight is found.

With puns that dive and punchlines reel,
The depth of laughter, it's quite the deal.
From light to dark, humor's a maze,
In every turn, we laugh for days.

So take a dip, don't hesitate,
The bottomless well will captivate.
For humor's tides will bring you cheer,
Refresh your spirit, dry that tear.

Lighthearted Crashes

He tripped on shoes that weren't his size,
A tumble down, much to our surprise.
The world spun fast, he made a face,
Laughter erupted, joy filled the space.

Each mishap, a reason to cheer,
As he bounces back, shedding fear.
Like a clown in a slapstick play,
Every crash turns blue skies to gray.

When he drops the pie, it's pure delight,
Fruit flies dance in comedic flight.
With each splatter, giggles resound,
In these blunders, laughter is found.

So let us cheer for every fall,
For in those moments, we find our call.
The joy of life in each silly clash,
In every misstep, lighthearted crashes.

The Sway of Silly Things

In a world of whims and funny knacks,
Where laughter wobbles and never lacks.
The moon might slip on a banana peel,
As our hearts for joy, we gladly deal.

Dancing socks on the floor will spin,
Chasing giggles, where fun begins.
With every swing, the world feels light,
Each silly twirl a pure delight.

Jokes that wobble, truths that sway,
In the tune of laughter, come what may.
Ticklish moments, brightening minds,
With every twist, we leave behind.

So sway with me, let's twirl and play,
In the rhythm of humor, we'll find our way.
For in the dance of the silly cling,
The joy of life is in the swing.

The Weight of Laughter

Laughter falls like feathers, oh so light,
Yet drops on toes—what a comical sight!
With each hearty chuckle, our ribs may shake,
But watch out for the cake, make no mistake!

In the court of joy, we plead the jest,
Where smiles are heavy and they jest!
A ticklish tease upon the floor,
We slip and slide, then laugh for more!

So pull a prank, let silliness reign,
For laughter's weight is our sweet gain.
What's light can tumble, what's heavy flies,
In this circus of joy, we reach for the skies!

While giggles tumble and mischief sparks,
The punchlines echo through the parks.
Let the humor drop like water balloons,
Every splash a note in our laughter tunes!

The Fallacy of Lightness

Flying high on hopes that feel so grand,
But down they come like castles of sand.
A whisper of joy, a tickled chuckle,
Do we float or fall? What a great shuffle!

In the dance of wit, we trip and sway,
Gravity's jest plays a cheeky display.
Light as a feather, heavy as a brick,
Life's funny paradoxes, oh, what a kick!

We bounce like balls when laughter ensues,
Each giggle is a flip, each snort a ruse.
So take a leap, let your worries go,
For what seems light can pack quite a show!

In this playful riddle, we spin and twirl,
With each little misstep, the laughter unfurls.
A paradox spins while we reel and roll,
Finding humor is the heart and soul!

When Tethers Tickled Tears

Bungee jumping into jokes unknown,
With every bounce, we claim our throne!
Tethers tickle like sneezes at night,
Pulling us up from our laughter flight.

Tears of joy stream down our cheeks,
As gravity leaves us laughing for weeks.
What a ride on a wave of glee,
As we soar and tumble, feel so free!

In the fickle winds of a punchline's cheer,
We cradle our giggles, hold them near.
Let the world around us spin and sway,
For laughter's grip is here to stay!

Tethers untwist; we risk a fall,
Yet every giggle is worth it all.
Laughter, our anchor, catches us tight,
In this wacky world, everything's light!

The Pull of Playful Paradoxes

In the land of paradox, we bounce and play,
Where silliness leads the serious astray.
A tug on the shirt, a switch of the hat,
What weighs us down is a laugh, imagine that!

A heavy blink, a light-hearted jest,
In every chortle, we find our rest.
The pull of hilarity spins us around,
As laughter lifts and tumbles the ground.

So dodge the mundane and leap with glee,
In the circus of wit, you're wild and free!
Silly slips and accidental gains,
Each giggle a win, lose your chains!

Dive into cheer, let the giggles ignite,
For it's in playful paradoxes we find the light.
Each laugh a tether, each pun a flight,
Trust in the fun, our hearts take the height!

The Dark Side of Delight

In the depths of a black hole,
Laughs bounce like a lost soul.
Clowns tumble through space, quite absurd,
Dancing in silence, not a sound heard.

A tickle from stars, oh so bright,
Comets slip on banana peels at night.
Dark matter giggles, elusive and sly,
While hopeful astronauts wave goodbye.

It's a cosmic joke of grand design,
With astronauts tripping on their own spine.
Laughter rings where the light's out,
In the universe, that's what it's about!

So hold on tight, don't lose your grip,
In this galaxy, take a wild trip.
For when you fall through, just be aware,
The punchlines land, with style and flair.

Tethered to the Punchline

A summer breeze tickles the air,
As laughter floats without a care.
Everyone's soaring, stuck in a loop,
Trying to catch the invisible troupe.

A jester on a tightrope, no net in sight,
Teetering on clouds, oh what a fright!
The punchlines dangle, like pies in the sky,
Do they land or vanish? Oh my, oh my!

Knotted in laughter, tied up in space,
Each giggle a tether, a playful trace.
In this show of charm, fun will arise,
With every wrong step, the crowd just complies.

So tip your hat to the stars above,
For gravity's jest is a gift of love.
As we slip and slide, let's all just chime,
In this cosmic circus, it's all just sublime.

The Sway of Silliness

A rubber chicken flies through the void,
As serious stargazers look quite annoyed.
Stars chuckle softly at their own grace,
While planets spin in a wobbly race.

Twinkling giggles tickle the night,
Asteroids dance to their own delight.
Jokes are tossed like confetti in space,
As silly rolls coalesce in a place.

A rocket fueled by laughter and cheer,
Launches the punchlines far and near.
Tumbling through space, we join the song,
With every blunder where we belong.

So grab a friend, hold on tight,
In the sway of silliness, take flight.
For when you float in joy's embrace,
Even the stars share a grin on their face.

Tides of Irony

As the universe spins with a wink,
Planets sip coffee, and stars blink.
Astrophysicists scribble down notes,
While space critters plot their silly quotes.

A black hole swirls with a chuckle so deep,
As cosmic ducks quack before they leap.
The irony's thick, like thick-glazed pie,
What pulls you in is a reason to fly.

Comets play tag, with a slippery grace,
While meteor showers fill up the space.
A giggling moon plays peek-a-boo bright,
Casting shadows that dance in the night.

So ride the waves of this cosmic jest,
Where daydreams and punchlines intertwine best.
For in the chaos of stars and tides,
Even the absurd in joy abides.

The Downfall of Dullness

In an elevator, dreams take flight,
But a full pizza drops, oh what a sight!
Splat on the floor, cheese looks so sad,
Dull moments vanish, we laugh like mad.

Boredom takes a twist, in a jolly way,
When a rubber chicken leads the ballet.
Slips and slides turn our frowns to grins,
Life's too short, let the laughter begin!

A pumpkin rolls, it's a smooth descent,
All while the cat looks quite nonchalant.
With a hilarious thud, our day revives,
Who knew dullness within could be alive?

So here's to the wobbly, the silly and bright,
Embrace the absurd, make it your light!
When life gets heavy, just dance and prance,
In the world's great jest, give laughter a chance.

A Giggle's Gravitational Field

Under the waning moon, we float and sway,
With giggles that bounce in a playful ballet.
A feathered cap dance, all dressed in cheer,
Tickling each other, no space for fear.

As jello wobbles on the table (oh dear!),
Each quake sends laughter, drawing us near.
The punchline swings round like a comet's tail,
In this playful cosmos, we never derail.

Juggling hopes and dreams with marshmallow ease,
A slip on the floor becomes quite the tease.
In unity, laughter defies all the toil,
Creating a world from our whimsical soil.

So let's float together in this joy-filled ride,
With giggles that soar, let's take on the tide.
A festival of chuckles, come join the spree,
In this field of laughter, we're wild and free.

The Laughable Brink

On the edge of the world, where silliness reigns,
A tightrope of giggles, where humor remains.
With banana peels laid in a precise arc,
Even the moon chuckles, lighting the dark.

A trampoline bounce sends us high in the air,
While a rubber fish flops, with nary a care.
Laughter emerges as we tumble and spin,
Finding joy in the clash, where lightness begins.

Each jest is a leap, each pun a grand dive,
On this brink of delight, we feel so alive.
A slip and a pardon, a grin on our face,
In the theatre of joy, we all find our place.

So tiptoe with laughter, take that bold step,
Where humor embraces, and life's full of pep.
The brink is our canvas, filled wide with cheer,
Where the tickles of joy can last through the year.

The Dance of Weightlessness

In a world full of giggles, we float up high,
With shoes made of pudding, under a smirked sky.
Spinning and swirling, we lose our ground,
While upside-down turtles are joyously found.

With every small bounce, the chuckles expand,
A jellybean jiggle: oh, isn't it grand?
Whirling like dervishes, all in a line,
We twirl through the air, making laughter divine.

A hiccup's a note in this cheerful ballet,
As jellyfish drift in a wobbly sway.
Gravity's quirks make our bodies so light,
In this moment of joy, everything feels right.

So join the escapade, lift spirits high,
On the dance floor of whimsy, let laughter comply.
With time slipping slowly, we chuckle and play,
In this dance of delight, all worries decay.

The Gravity of Wit

In a world where jokes ascend,
Laughter floats, it knows no end.
But when it lands with just a thud,
You realize humor's stuck in mud.

A banana peel on the floor,
Waiting for feet to slip once more.
Doc says it's all in good fun,
But the giggles weigh a ton!

Caught in a Cosmic Chuckle

Stars are winking in delight,
As I stargaze into the night.
The universe plays tricks on me,
With every punchline, oh so free!

Planets roll their comic eyes,
While comets shoot with goofy sighs.
But if I fall from a shooting star,
I hope to land where laughs are far!

The Pull of Punchlines

In the orbit of a clever jest,
The best ideas collide, no rest.
The laughter pulls me near, it's true,
A soft landing, who knew?

Circling around a humor moon,
My sides will ache, I'll howl and croon.
But when the punchline hits the ground,
I'll roll in mirth, who'd have thought it found?

Falling Up: A Comedic Tale

I jumped on clouds, trying to fly,
But gravity grinned, oh my, oh my!
I soared through laughter, hit a joke,
Only to land where the punchlines poke.

With every tumble, I gain some cheer,
As giggles chase me, drawing near.
And though my feet are bound to trip,
My heart floats high on this comedy ship.

Kites of Wit in Stormy Skies

Kites dance wildly in the breeze,
Chasing clouds with giggles and ease.
One took a dive, what a sight!
Laughter echoed through the twilight.

Strings got tangled, a comic mess,
Floating high, the kites confess.
Wind whispers secrets, playful and sly,
As laughter sparkles in the sky.

The ground looks up, in pure surprise,
At kites that plot their silly guise.
Wit takes flight, above it all,
With wings of humor, we stand tall.

Dance, dear kites, embrace the gale,
For in each twist, you tell a tale.
Laughter's the anchor; let it hold,
As stormy skies become pure gold.

The Drift of Drollery

Floating thoughts on breezy air,
Tickling fancies, light as a hair.
Fell off the shelf, that book of jests,
Now laughter lingers in all the crests.

Jokes sail by on feathered wings,
Bouncing off clouds, oh how it sings!
Each pun a puff, so light, so spry,
We giggle and fall as we drift high.

In this realm of wit and cheer,
Every burst of fun draws us near.
Ticklish breezes push and pull,
In this drift, our hearts are full.

When mirth takes hold, what a delight,
As whimsy dances into the night.
We ride the waves of chuckles shared,
In the drift of drollery, joy's ensnared.

Broken Gravity

Falling sideways, what a view!
Upside down, our laughter grew.
The moon wore shoes, how absurdly bright,
As comedy twisted throughout the night.

Jokes dropped like feathers to the floor,
Each silly quip opened a door.
In this tumble, we find our play,
Where funny rules and quirks display.

Laughter bounces without a care,
Defying logic, floating in air.
Every misstep, a giggling spree,
In broken poise, we're all set free.

What a joke, this dance of jest!
In topsy-turvy, we're truly blessed.
So here's to the silly, embrace the glee,
In broken realms, we find our spree.

Woken Joy

Awake with smiles, the day begins,
Chasing shadows, shedding sins.
Joy bounces like a ball, so spry,
In the morning light, we laugh and fly.

With silly hats and socks askew,
We dance in circles, me and you.
Each giggle bursts like morning dew,
As sunshine blinks, bright and true.

Jokes pop out like toast, so warm,
In this playful world, we find our charm.
Every moment spins on fun,
Woken joy, our hearts are one.

So let us leap and twirl about,
In this crazy game, there's no doubt.
With laughter loud, our spirits soar,
In woken joy, we crave for more.

When Words Take Flight

Words take stickers, fly so high,
With silly shapes, they whirl and sigh.
Each phrase a rocket, blasting cheer,
In a universe where jokes appear.

Double entendres, sly and spry,
Twirl like feathers across the sky.
In every pun, we find our wings,
As laughter blooms and softly sings.

Whimsical thoughts on breezes glide,
Chasing dreams, we turn the tide.
In this sky of fun, let's unite,
When words take flight, our hearts ignite.

So let's release our ties to ground,
Float away where joy is found.
With every quip, we soar and beam,
In this flight of words, we chase a dream.

When Stars Take a Spill

Stars giggle as they slip,
Over cosmic banana peels,
They twirl in a glitzy trip,
Dancing on the darkened reels.

Planets chuckle, burst and spin,
As confetti asteroids fly,
With a wink, they dive right in,
In the night, they laugh and sigh.

Galaxies wobble, sway about,
Making jokes in stellar bounds,
Spinning tales without a doubt,
Echoes of their gleeful sounds.

Clouds of dust, they roll and play,
Across the universe so wide,
When stars take a tumble, hey,
All of space becomes a ride!

The Weight of Laughter

Laughter floats like bubbles bright,
Defying all that pulls us down,
With every giggle, pure delight,
It's weightless humor we have found.

Tickles race through every space,
As chuckles echo without end,
A silly grin, a playful chase,
From little quirks, we will ascend.

Banana peels on comets glide,
With every slip comes joy's embrace,
In the cosmos, joy won't hide,
For smiles dance in every place.

Come, take a ride on laughter's beam,
Light as air, so free and spry,
In this realm, we live the dream,
With humor lifting to the sky!

The Fall that Lifts Us

Down we tumble, oh what fun,
Like clowns with shoes that simply slip,
Falling gently, one by one,
We catch ourselves in laughter's grip.

Every trip that we make here,
Transforms the ground to joyful heights,
In every tumble, shout and cheer,
As giggles light up starry nights.

When we drop, the smiles arise,
Like balloons that softly soar,
Each stumble is a grand surprise,
Who knew the ground could be a floor?

Rolling down this hill of glee,
With every fumble, hearts will sing,
The fall that lifts us, wild and free,
Shows us what true joy can bring!

Anchored to the Sky

With goofy hats and silly sighs,
We float like leaves up in the trees,
Tethered not by weight or ties,
But by laughter carried by the breeze.

Balloons bob high with each joke,
As comets laugh past twinkling light,
Even the moon, it starts to poke,
And join the fun with sheer delight.

Up above, the universe grins,
Each star a partner in the jest,
When laughter falls, it always wins,
Anchored high, it's simply the best.

So let us drift in this grand dance,
With smiles that never truly fade,
In this skyward, joyous prance,
Together in the fun we've made!

The Lean of Laughter

When the squirrel slipped on a fruit,
He dashed down, all limbs in pursuit.
With a thud that echoed in glee,
Even the tree laughed, 'Oh, look at thee!'

On the tightrope, a juggler swayed,
His balls arched high, oh what a cascade!
One slipped and knocked off his hat,
The crowd roared, 'Was that planned, or what?'

A cat on a fence tried a leap,
Over the dog, her heart took a sweep.
Alas! She landed on the grass,
The dog wagged his tail, as if to pass.

In a universe where smiles collide,
Every tumble gets perfect pride.
With each blunder, a cheer will ring,
For laughter is nature's finest fling.

Cosmic Follies

In space, a peanut lost its way,
It floated off—'Not this, not today!'
A comet winked, 'You lost your spark,'
The peanut replied, 'It's just a lark.'

The stars had a dance-off one night,
They twirled and spun, oh what a sight!
But one star tripped on its bright tail,
And fell down with a glittery wail.

Aliens peeked through their green lens,
Said, 'Earthlings dance like they have no sense!'
Yet on their world, they slipped on cheese,
And rolled 'round laughing, 'Oh, bring us ease!'

The moon chuckled, his glow growing wide,
As planets embraced in a giggling glide.
For in this cosmic comedy show,
Even the suns know how to throw.

Laughter's Embrace

A frog on a lily pad slipped, oh dear,
He leapt to the left, then toppled—oh, sheer!
The pond burst with echoes of mirth,
As fish swam by, 'What a jump, what a berth!'

A snail with dreams walked a long line,
He cried, 'I'll get there; just give me some time!'
But then he tripped on his own shell,
And laughed at himself, 'Well, all's well!'

The mice planned a feast of grand scale,
But cheese rolled away, following the trail.
They chased in a frenzy, hearts full of cheer,
What a funny buffet, let's grab some beer!

Under the moonlight where giggles reside,
Joy dances in shadows, lets worries slide.
For in every stumble, in every embrace,
Laughter's the magic that fills up the space.

The Fickle Nature of Air

A balloon drifted up with a sigh,
But wind gave a tickle, and oh my, oh my!
It spun and it twirled like a silly kite,
Then popped with a laugh—oh what a fright!

The feather floated down soft and slow,
But carried by gusts, began its show.
It tickled a dog right on the nose,
Sending him bouncing—his laughter arose!

A kite soared high above the park,
With a tail that fluttered like a lark.
But a sudden gust sent it tumbling low,
The kids on the ground just started to glow.

In each twist of air, there's a jest,
Where even the clouds can't help but jest.
And when we fall, how we land with flair,
Remind us that laughter is always in air.

Sinking into Whimsy

In the realm where laughter gleams,
Jokes fall down like playful dreams.
Each slip and trip a funny fate,
As we stumble, we celebrate.

Floating high on giddy air,
With silly jokes that seem to dare.
A punch that lands, we burst with glee,
As hilarity sets us free.

Laughter rolls like a cosmic tide,
With punchlines pulling us to ride.
Down we go, but smiles remain,
In the spiral of joyful pain.

From the stars to the ground,
The giggles echo all around.
Each bounce and fall, a sweet delight,
In this universe of light.

The Orbit of Quips

In a loop where puns revolve,
Laughter finds the quirks to solve.
Jokes zipping round like comets bright,
We chase them down, what a sight!

The witty pull, we can't resist,
With every twist, we laugh and twist.
A satirical spin, a jolly game,
Each punchline makes the heart aflame.

Ever circling in mirth,
Where every quip is of great worth.
Round and round, we catch the thrill,
As joy ignites, we can't sit still.

With humor's force, we take a stand,
Gravity loves a playful hand.
So let's bust a gut with all our might,
In this orbit of sheer delight.

A Spiral of Smiles

In a twirl of grins and cheer,
Laughter whispers in our ear.
The world spins in a silly way,
As we embrace this funny sway.

Round we go, the jokes do flow,
A scene that blooms where giggles grow.
With every chuckle, we dive deep,
Into the joy that we can keep.

Lively jests collide with grace,
A cosmic dance in open space.
A tumble here, a joke, a grin,
The spiral twirls, we dive right in.

With smiles bright, we fly so high,
In this zany, boundless sky.
Together we laugh, together we play,
In the spiral that won't fade away.

The Universe Tickled

Among the stars, a laugh takes flight,
In a cosmos painted with delight.
With each starburst, a chuckle shines,
In the universe, where humor entwines.

Planets wobble on a punny quest,
As giggles echo, a welcome jest.
The milky way is all a tumble,
Where we laugh and joyfully jumble.

Witty comets streak the night,
Creating trails of sheer delight.
Laughter bursts like supernovas bright,
In this dance of cosmic light.

Through black holes and playful spins,
The universe knows where laughter begins.
So let us float on this merry ride,
And chase the joy that won't subside.

Jokes from the Abyss

Why did the stone feel great?
It finally met its fate!
Falling down with a sly grin,
Told the world, 'I just took a spin!'

Why did the apple lose its core?
It couldn't take the weight anymore!
With a thud it made a scene,
Said, 'I'm just too ripe and green!'

Why did the comet start to dance?
It couldn't miss the downward chance!
With a twirl and a joyful loop,
It landed in a cosmic scoop!

So when you trip on your own two feet,
Just remember it's a gravity feat!
Life's a joke that can take a fall,
With laughter echoing through it all!

When the Earth Laughs

Why did the moon chuckle so light?
It saw the sun slip from its height!
As the world had a silly trip,
The stars all did a funny flip!

Why did the hill start to tease?
It saw a tumble that was sure to please!
A rock rolled down with such a flair,
Shouting, 'Watch me, if you dare!'

What did the clouds say when they fell?
'It's not the end, just a cascade yell!'
Among the raindrops, giggles poured,
As every drop fell with a hoard!

So listen close when the earth sighs,
It's just a punchline in disguise!
Each little stumble, every trip,
Is nature's way of sharing a skip!

Punchlines from Below

Did you hear the boulder joke?
It cracked up and nearly broke!
'Tell me why I roll,' said it,
'Because being still—it's just not it!'

Why did the puddle start to laugh?
It knew its fate was a silly path!
Surprised by feet that dance in range,
It giggled, 'Oh, let's rearrange!'

What did the earthworms do with cheer?
They wiggled out to hear the cheer!
'Each drop we take is quite the show,
Just watch as we steal the flow!'

So take a fall and fall with glee,
Let the punchlines set you free!
For in the tumble, you'll see the fun,
As laughter dances with each run!

A Lightness in the Drop

Why did the feather feel so bold?
It took a dive straight from the cold!
Said, 'Every fall makes me feel bright,
As I twirl in the playful light!'

Why did the leaf swirl around?
It giggled as it hit the ground!
Each fluttered laugh, a gentle tease,
Wanted to share its joyful breeze!

What did the raindrop shout out loud?
'I'm falling free, no reason to crowd!'
With each plop and playful splatter,
It shared its joy, nothing could matter!

So when you plummet, take delight,
In every falling moment bright!
Life's a quip that can take a shot,
Embrace the drop, it's quite the plot!

www.ingramcontent.com/pod-product-compliance
Lightning Source LLC
Chambersburg PA
CBHW051629160426
43209CB00004B/576